COMMUNITY CONNECTIONS **?**

WHAT DOES IT DO?
TRACTOR

BY JOSH GREGORY

CHERRY
LAKE
Publishing

Published in the United States of America by Cherry Lake Publishing
Ann Arbor, Michigan
www.cherrylakepublishing.com

Content Adviser: Louis Teel, Professor of Heavy Equipment, Central Arizona College
Reading Adviser: Cecilia Minden-Cupp, PhD, Literacy Consultant

Photo Credits: Cover and page 1, ©Nanostock/Shutterstock, Inc.; page 5, ©Tom
Biegalski/Shutterstock, Inc.; page 7, ©Jim Parkin/Shutterstock, Inc.; page 9, ©Nate A./
Shutterstock, Inc.; page 11, ©EMJAY SMITH/Shutterstock, Inc.; page 13, ©iStockphoto.com/
alexandrupetrache; page 15, ©Grant Heilman Photography/Alamy; page 17, ©iStockphoto.com/
SusanHSmith; page 19, ©iStockphoto.com/tsz01; page 21, ©Darryl Vest/Shutterstock, Inc.

LIBRARY OF CONGRESS CATALOGING-IN-PUBLICATION DATA
Gregory, Josh.
  What does it do? Tractor/by Josh Gregory.
    p. cm.—(Community connections)
  Includes bibliographical references and index.
  ISBN-13: 978-1-60279-970-7 (lib. bdg.)
  ISBN-10: 1-60279-970-9 (lib. bdg.)
  1. Tractors—Juvenile literature. I. Title. II. Title: Tractor. III. Series.
  TL233.15.G74 2010
  631.3'72—dc22   2010023546

Cherry Lake Publishing would like to acknowledge the
work of The Partnership for 21st Century Skills. Please
visit www.21stcenturyskills.org for more information.

Printed in the United States of America
Corporate Graphics Inc.
January 2011
CLSP08

TRACTOR

CONTENTS

WHAT DOES IT DO?

ON THE FARM

Tractors are great machines. They push or pull special tools. Some tractors have tools connected to them that push snow. Other tools clear away dirt.

Tractors are important farm helpers. Have you ever seen a farm? Maybe you spotted fields of corn or bean plants. Farmers grow the plants. They **harvest** the **crops**.

Some farms stretch as far as the eye can see.

How can farmers raise so many crops? They use tractors to get a lot of the work done. Before tractors, farmers used horses for some jobs. Horses pulled **plows** and other tools. Tractors helped change farming.

Today, there are fewer farmers, but they are raising more crops. Tractors help make this possible.

Horses are strong, but tractors are faster.

What do horses need to stay healthy? Think about it. What do horses need that tractors do not? Horses can get tired if they work too long. Do tractors get tired? What are other reasons to use tractors instead of horses?

7

Tractors are slower than cars. They are more powerful, though.

Farm tractors often have large tires. They help tractors drive through mud.

Tractors can also pull heavy machines behind them. Farmers use tractors to move things around, too.

A tractor is one of a farmer's most important tools.

TRACTOR TOOLS

Tractors need help from other machines to do many jobs. These machines or tools connect to the tractor.

Some machines help a farmer cut hay or dig up weeds. Other machines plant seeds in fields.

Machines can be connected to the front or back of a tractor.

Getting the soil ready for planting is important. Can you guess what helps farmers do this job? Tractors!

Tractors help **till** the soil. The machine pulls a plow. The plow turns over the soil and breaks it into chunks. Other tools break up the dirt chunks into smaller bits.

Farmers use plows to get fields ready for planting.

Tractors can pull **seeders**. These machines quickly plant hundreds of seeds.

Some farmers use food **plot** seeders. These machines turn the soil and plant seeds at the same time. These helpful tools are hooked to the tractor.

Seeders help farmers plant lots of seeds at once.

Do you live near any
farms? Ask a parent
to take you to one.
Be sure to visit when
farmers are working.
Is anyone using a
tractor? Is the tractor
pulling a machine?
How is the tractor
helping the farmer
do her job?

15

Imagine running older tractors. They were loud and shaky. Would you want to use one for very long?

Important changes have made new tractors much nicer. They have comfortable seats. Many have air-conditioning and are not as loud. Drivers have more room. These changes help farmers stay on their tractors longer and finish their work faster.

Farmers spend a lot of time in their tractors.

MAKE A GUESS!

Can you guess why people must keep tractors in good shape? Would tractors work well if they had broken parts? Could they be less safe to use?

17

Farmers need to be careful when using tractors. Tractors have many moving parts and can tip over. People can get hurt if they get too close. Tractors must always be kept in good shape.

Safety is important when working with big machines such as tractors!

TRACTORS AT HOME

Farmers aren't the only people who use tractors. Workers use different tractors to help build houses or roads. You may even have a tractor at home. Do your parents cut the grass with a lawn mower they sit on? That lawn mower is a small tractor!

Now you know more about what tractors do. They are busy machines!

Some people use small tractors to mow their lawns.

GLOSSARY

crops (KROPSS) plants grown by farmers, usually for food

harvest (HAR-vist) to pick or gather crops

plot (PLOT) a small area of land

plows (PLOUZ) tools that are pulled by tractors to break up soil

seeders (SEE-durz) machines that are pulled by tractors to plant seeds

till (TIL) to mix up and break hard chunks of soil

FIND OUT MORE

BOOKS

Glover, David, and Penny Glover. *Tractors in Action*. New York: PowerKids Press, 2008.

Tourville, Amanda Doering. *Tractors*. Edina, MN: Magic Wagon, 2009.

WEB SITES

Deere & Company—Johnny Tractor and His Pals
www.deere.com/en_US/compinfo/kidscorner/johnnypalstory.html
Read a fun story about a tractor and other farm machines.

KidsHealth—Farm Safety
kidshealth.org/kid/watch/out/farm_safety.html
Learn how to stay safe around tractors and other machines.

INDEX

ABOUT THE AUTHOR

Josh Gregory writes and edits books for kids. He lives in Chicago, Illinois.